John Frade

12/2022

IMAGES
of America

SHERIDAN

IMAGES
of America

SHERIDAN

Pat Blair, Dana Prater, and
the Sheridan County Museum

ARCADIA
PUBLISHING

*To the current and former boards and staffs of the Sheridan
County Historical Society and the Sheridan County Fulmer
Public Library, Wyoming Room, who have preserved Sheridan's
history for our community's present and future generations.*

CONTENTS

ACKNOWLEDGMENTS

The authors would like to thank the Sheridan County Historical Society Museum for making its photographic collection available and the board of directors for allowing its use.

Many thanks are due the Sheridan community who donated images for the Sheridan County Memory Book Project, and sponsors ERA Carroll Realty and the Homer A. and Mildred S. Scott Foundation. Photographs from the following Memory Book Project donors were used to help illustrate Sheridan's history: Tim Barnes, Barb Brettin, Scott Burgan for Glenn Sweem, Marilyn Bilyeu for Elsa Spear Byron, Marc Coffeen, Scott Davis, Byron Elmgren, Dr. George Ewan, Fuller Studio/Camera West and Dick Kehrwald, Beth Garbutt, Deanna George, Prudence Grunkemeyer, Libby Gwinn, Jean Harm, Stu Healy, Mary Holstedt, Janet Holcomb, Sharon Humphrey, Janet Kilpatrick for Stanley Kuzara, Dorothy King, Mark Kinner, Miff Koltiska, Dick Lenz, Laura MacCarty, Sam and Lynn Mavrakis, Joe and Rene Meyer, Doris Moeller-Edwards, LaVonne Nelson, Anita Nichols, Marsha Masters Powers, Ann Garbutt Ryan, Lyndon Schwamb, Sheridan Fire Rescue, Kurt Smith, Steve Songer, Darcy Taylor, Robert H. Walsh, Alice Warnke, Lucille White, and Bill Wondra. Unless otherwise noted, all photographs are from the Sheridan County Museum and the Sheridan County Library's Wyoming Room collections.

The staff of the Wyoming Room of the Sheridan County Fulmer Public Library was also (as always) extremely helpful. Karen Woinoski, Andy Wenburg, and Sylvia Hodges ably assisted us with our search. Many thanks to the donors who contributed to the Wyoming Room's collections that were used in this publication. These include Alan Bourne, Myrtle Brockett, Elsa Spear Byron, Don Diers, Wayne and Betty Dygert, Dr. George Ewan, Robert and Mary Holstedt, Anna Kelly, Margaret Lansing, Clarice Kerr Lugenbeel, the Thomas T. Tynan family, Jack and Connie Wilson, and the Wyoming Room Collections.

Proceeds from the sale of this book will benefit the Sheridan County Historical Society Museum, and we appreciate the museum's staff, Nathan Doerr, Valarie Krecker, and museum advisor, Jeffrey C. Prater, Ph.D.

Regretfully, size and space limitations do not allow the inclusion of every great photograph or tidbit of Sheridan history. The responsibility for any errors or omissions rests with the authors.

INTRODUCTION

The story of Sheridan, Wyoming, takes the archetypal American frontier experience and transforms it into something unique. Many of the traditional elements of western settlement are there, to be sure, but a legacy of special circumstances gives the community a distinct flavor of bygone days. Indeed, a combination of historic buildings, a strong sense of heritage, and good old western hospitality convinced *True West* editor Bob Boze Bell that Sheridan would be the magazine's first recipient of its annual No. 1 Western Town in America Award. The spitting image of George Armstrong Custer leading the 7th Cavalry Drum and Bugle Corps dressed in 1870s-era army uniforms no doubt cinched the deal for Bell.

From the beginning, the indigenous peoples and their European and American successors, in turn, found a bountiful land nestled on the eastern slope of the Big Horn Mountains. Each group was determined to possess the area, so cultural conflict was inevitable. The Crows were the most prominent of the American Indian tribes and derived their name from a trapper's rough translation of *Apsaalooke*, or "children of the large beaked bird." Absaroka (the Land of the Crows) caught the of eye of other tribes, however, and before long, the Lakota and Northern Cheyenne tribes began forcibly moving in from the east, becoming hated enemies of the Crow.

By 1866, white incursions along the latest road to the Montana goldfields, the Bozeman Trail, threatened the new Lakota/Cheyenne hunting grounds, and Oglala chief Red Cloud initiated a series of bloody contests later known as the Great Sioux Wars. The first major battle occurred in December 1866 when Capt. William J. Fetterman and his command were lured into an ambush. Before reinforcements from Fort Phil Kearny could arrive, all 83 men were annihilated. The subsequent Laramie Treaty of 1868 forced the withdrawal of whites from the "unceded territory" and established the nearby Crow Reservation.

Peace proved fragile, however, as unsuccessful federal efforts to secure the Black Hills prompted the Centennial Campaign of 1876. The Lakota and Northern Cheyenne tribes faced blue-coated soldiers and their Crow and Shoshone allies in a series of campaigns throughout 1876 and 1877. The former achieved noteworthy successes—first against Gen. George Crook at the Battle of the Rosebud in June 1876 and then against Col. George Armstrong Custer at Little Big Horn a week later. Despite these achievements, the tribes eventually succumbed, and the area opened to white settlement a short time later.

One particularly attractive portion of land around Little and Big Goose Creeks lured former members of Crook's campaign back to the area they had dubbed Camp Cloud Peak. Ranchers, cowboys, homesteaders, and merchants flocked to the area as well. George Mandel operated a post office in a little cabin where the Rock Creek stage line crossed Big Goose Creek. A cabin built in 1878 by trapper Dutch Henry was nearby, along with a barn that housed horses for stage-line teams. These people and these three buildings would be the nucleus of an emerging town. By 1882, John D. Loucks had bought the Mandel place, become postmaster, and commenced sketching out a town on brown wrapping paper. He wrote the name Sheridan at the top for his Civil War commander, convinced that he had chosen exactly the right place for a prosperous town.

This is an attempt to sketch the colorful history of Sheridan in the following pages using photographs from various archival collections. These are arranged topically and reflect, in broad strokes, a portion of the area's history. Generally speaking, Sheridan's immigrants either brought their trades with them or adapted their skills and special talents to the unique challenges and opportunities of the Big Horn country. Several different cultures met in Sheridan, creating a melting pot of people. Whether they were ranchers, businessmen, miners, or railroaders, of English nobility, European descent, or Americans of all varieties, they came to this area to realize their dreams in the West.

One

THE FIRST
40 ACRES

On the eve of becoming the county seat of the newly formed Sheridan County in 1888, the town of Sheridan was just six years old. Founded by John Loucks in 1882, the future town was already populated by ranchers, cowboys, and homesteaders who entered the area a few years after the resolution of American Indian conflicts in 1876. Like most towns in the West, Sheridan had its compliment of hotels, liveries, saloons, shops for dry goods, millinery, drugs, lumber, a Chinese laundry, and two newspapers. The Windsor Hotel is the large building on the left and was one of the town's social centers. The importance of Sheridan's selection as the county seat would have crucial benefits in the years to come, as would Sheridan's selection as the route for the Burlington and Missouri River Railroad.

By the time this photograph was taken in 1889, more than 50 buildings occupied the town. When John Loucks arrived to visit his friend James Works in 1882, he found George Mandel's post office in a little cabin where the Rock Creek stage line crossed Big Goose Creek. An old cabin built in 1878 by a trapper known as Dutch Henry was nearby, along with a horse barn for the stage-line teams. These buildings would be the nucleus of the emerging town.

James Works convinced John Loucks to stay, and Loucks purchased George Mandel's cabin and claim for $50 and traveled south to find a justice of the peace so he could be sworn in as postmaster. On his way back, Loucks stopped to rest on what is now Courthouse Hill. Enthralled by the abundant grass and grazing herds of buffalo and deer, he returned to the cabin and sketched out the town of his dreams on a piece of brown wrapping paper. He named the town for his Civil War commander, Gen. Philip Sheridan.

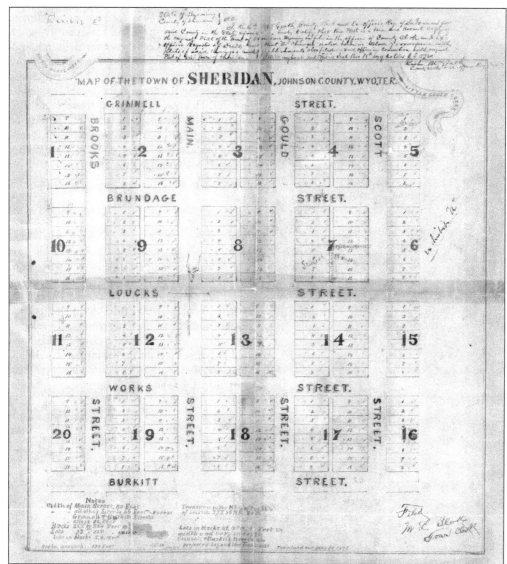

On May 10, 1882, John Loucks contacted engineer Jack Dow of neighboring Big Horn City to survey the 40-acre town. Streets were named after several men who had already taken up claims in the area and helped with the survey: Kenneth Burkitt, James Works, George Brundage, Alexander Gould, L. H. Brooks, and W. Scott, who served as secretary and treasurer of the newly formed town company. For some reason early on, Grinnell Street was changed to Smith Street, and Grinnell Street, named for local rancher Cornelius H. Grinnell, was moved one block to the north. Corner lots in the 40-acre town were $5, and inside lots were sold for $3. This is an official copy of the original plat filed in Johnson County, Wyoming Territory, in 1892.

Henry Held was another of Sheridan's earliest townsmen. Held was heading for the Yellowstone country when he pulled up his wagon to stay overnight in brand-new Sheridan. When John Loucks found out that the new arrival was a blacksmith, he made Dutch Henry's trapper cabin available, and Held set up his shop there. Held filed a claim on adjacent land and purchased lots in Sheridan where he built his new blacksmith shop on the northwest corner of Main and Works Streets.

Henry Held's blacksmith shop was the first structure built on the new Main Street in 1882. Henry Neitman (right) purchased Held's shop in the 1890s. Held also built the town's first irrigation ditch that can be seen in many of the photographs, developed one of the earliest subdivisions, and helped build the first electric light plant in Sheridan. He later donated land for the city cemetery. Held passed away in 1934.

An inscription on this photograph by Henry Held's wife, Nettie, indicates that this may be Dutch Henry's cabin that Held used for a blacksmith shop. After Held moved to his new shop on Main Street, John Loucks moved the Dutch Henry cabin next to the Mandel cabin, where it remained for about six months. The cabins served as the location for the first Christmas party, school, election, and home for Loucks's wife and two children. In 1883, Loucks moved the Mandel cabin to the northwest corner of Main and Loucks Streets, where it was enlarged and used for Loucks's store and home. The Dutch Henry cabin stayed where it was, and after being used as an icehouse for a while, the cabin was dismantled.

In 1884, Henry Held built this home for his wife, Nettie, and their daughter, Birdie, directly across Main Street from his blacksmith shop. The Helds owned several lots in town and moved to another house on Gould Street just a few years later. This home has been enlarged and used for many different businesses over the years and still stands at the northeast corner of South Main and Works Streets.

Built in 1882, the Cow Boy Saloon lasted briefly at the southwest corner of Main and Loucks Streets. Its patrons included the area's first inhabitants, shown here, and the saloon's proprietors were Pete Jones and Jim Morrow. After a few years, the building became a drugstore and can be seen in several of the following photographs. Its last use was as a tire store, and it was torn down in 1925 to make way for an impressive bank, which still stands on the location.

Sheridan was founded in the middle of a good grazing area, somewhat to the consternation of area ranchers. In this 1885 photograph by J. Dalgleish of Buffalo, Wyoming, men of the Cross Cattle Company cut hay on land where the Sheridan Inn would be built several years later. These men became bankers, ranch owners, and the town's leading businessmen, including W. G. Griffen, Frank McCoy, Dave Dunnuck, C. W. Garbutt, and H. C. Alger.

John H. Conrad, the former post trader at nearby Fort McKinney, built this store across from the Cow Boy Saloon on Main Street in 1883. Conrad's carried everything from knitting needles to threshing machines. In later years, the building housed Hanna and Henschke's Groceries, Mrs. P. A. Campbell's Millinery, and Dan's Western Wear. Sheridan's third oldest building still stands at the northeast corner of Main and Loucks Streets and has housed the Hospital Pharmacy since the 1980s.

The Grand Central was Sheridan's first hotel, built by Dick Reed Sr. at the southeast corner of Main and Works Streets. All of Sheridan's townspeople—17 women and some 65 men—attended the opening ball on July 3, 1883. It was built with local lumber, and its fixtures and glass windows were hauled from Rock Creek, the Union Pacific railroad station in southern Wyoming. The nine-room hotel was replaced by the Keenan Building in 1914.

In this 1901 photograph, Sheridan businessmen B. F. Perkins and Edward A. Whitney stand in front of Sheridan's first bank. Whitney purchased John Loucks's cabin store at the corner of Main and Loucks Streets, added the clapboard siding and other improvements, and opened the Bank of Sheridan in 1885. Whitney invested in local ranches, served as the town's mayor, founded the state's first savings and loan, and established Whitney Benefits, a trust that has provided more than $50 million in student loans and community enhancements.

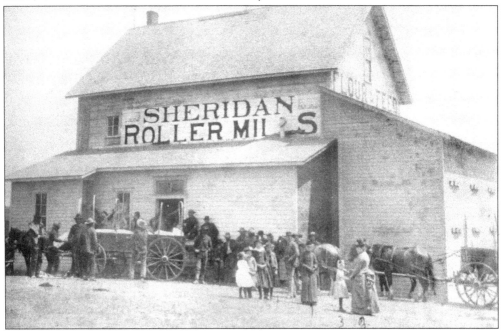

The Sheridan Roller Mills was built on the banks of Big Goose Creek in 1887 and supplied flour and cattle feeds. Aggie Mills, in the white dress, appears again. Her father was one of the mill's stockholders. Later enlarged and called the Sheridan Manufacturing Company, the mill was torn down in 1962 when flood-control projects redirected both Big and Little Goose Creeks.

The Sheridan Brewing Company was founded by Arnold Tschirgi, George Paul, and Peter Demple in 1887 and distributed its first product in 1888. The much-anticipated brewery survived robbers' intent on capturing the business's start-up funds. Instead of transporting the $10,000 in gold by way of the holdup-prone Cheyenne stage, the brewers avoided the thieves by taking the Northern Pacific Railroad to Custer Station, then transporting their capital the rest of the way by wagon.

Peter Demple had been a member of King Frederick's Bavarian army before coming to the United States in 1880. His talents were not confined to brewing, and in 1888, a building he constructed was used for the new Sheridan County Courthouse at the southeast corner of Main and Grinnell Streets. Later a number of businesses flourished there. It was torn down in the 1960s to make way for a Woolworth's store.

Seventeen students attended school in John Loucks's cabin, and the first frame school was built in 1884 on the northeast corner of Loucks and Gould Streets, the site of the current Sheridan Post Office. Built at a cost of $1,000, Loucks contributed the extra $200 for the bell and belfry. A brick schoolhouse joined the frame building a few years later, and both were known as the Central School before being replaced in 1920.

Sheridan's Masonic Lodge organized in 1886 and included leading Sheridan businessmen. Their first lodge meetings were held on the second floor of this building at the southwest corner of Main and Brundage Streets. Members were, from left to right, Samuel Atkinson, J. F. Hoop, C. W. Garbutt, F. E. Wunderlich, J. D. Loucks, C. W. Morgareidge, W. S. Metz, Dr. B. F. Kuney, W. G. Griffen, E. E. Lonabaugh, George H. Purmort, W. J. Stover, unidentified, Henry Held, Charles Sommers, unidentified, J. C. Bishop, unidentified, C. E. Peoples, S. H. Smith, and J. B. Moore.

The Windsor Hotel was built on the southwest corner of South Main and Works Streets in 1887. Robert J. Mills was the hotel manager and is pictured here with other town notables. His daughter, Aggie, is seen next to her father at the corner of the building. The Windsor Hotel was torn down in 1896 and replaced by a brick structure, the Hotel Towns, later known as the Great Western Hotel.

Built in 1888, this shopping block was on the southeast corner of North Main Street and Smith Alley. The businesses are, from left to right, J. Frank Heald's Jewelry Store, the Pioneer Restaurant, and Eads Harness and Saddlery, owned by Sheridan's first saddler, Andrew Eads. Henry Gerdle's store for ladies shoes is on the right. J. Frank Heald and Tom Tynan are in the buggy. Barrels sunk in the ditches on either side of Main Street provided water for firefighting.

The E. L Mills Stationery and Drug Company occupied the ground floor of the building at the northwest corner of Main and Brundage Streets. John Loucks and attorney Thomas Cotton began Sheridan's first newspaper, the *Sheridan Post*, on the second floor in 1887. In 1890, the building caught fire, and its contents were so carefully removed and saved by the ladies of the Methodist church that the insurance company rewarded them by donating a bell for the new church.

Henry Coffeen organized the first fair in Sheridan at the original fairgrounds south of town near Little Goose Creek. Livestock and agricultural shows were a big part of the fair, as was horse racing, probably the most popular event. The rail around the track is visible at far left. S. N. "Vess" Hardee, who homesteaded on Big Goose Creek in 1884, was known for his prized thoroughbreds.

The large building in the center was new in 1888 on the west side of Main Street between Works and Loucks Streets. Businesses included the Windsor Hotel, Henry Held's Blacksmith shop, the Sheridan Enterprise office, Arctic Saloon, Leaverton and Small's Drygoods, E. W. Scott Cigars, and Sheridan Drugs, formerly the Cow Boy Saloon. Dr. W. F. Green was Sheridan's first doctor, and with doctor and pharmacist Frank Kuney, ran Sheridan Drugs for many years.

The same view was taken in the mid-1890s and included the Congregational Church tower, Windsor Hotel, Henry Held's Blacksmith shop, the Hop Sing Chinese Laundry, the Sheridan Enterprise office, Arctic Saloon, Leaverton and Small's Drygoods, E. W. Scott Cigars, and Sheridan Drugs, formerly the Cow Boy Saloon. Leaverton and Small's second story housed Sheridan city government offices, and the post office used the building for three years, from 1907 to 1910.

21

Several groups were photographed in front of the Windsor Hotel on Decoration Day, 1888, possibly also celebrating Sheridan's selection as the new county seat. Sheridan beat out nearby communities Big Horn and Dayton for the honor, and residents were already certain that the Burlington and Missouri River Railroad would favor Sheridan in the next several years. Sheridan's women and children, including Aggie Mills (no. 8), posed for the camera that day.

Grand Army of the Republic Veterans gathered on the same day, including founding father John Loucks (with the white beard at center). Other members were Henry Held, J. Coursey, John Schuler, James K. P. Leaverton, Valentine Reece, James W. F. Ferguson, Cornelius Boulware, Dr. Benjamin F. Kuney, Jeremiah Murphy, James H. Buckley, Robert A. Moon, B. F. Martin, Pulaski Calvert, A. L. Bishop, William D. Wrighter, and William Denne.

The Sheridan Cornet Band formed in April 1888 and performed for the Decoration Day festivities that year. Band members are, from left to right, (seated) J. Frank Heald, Herbert Coffeen, Tom Tynan, Harry Neely, and Charles Thurmond; (second row) Mike Burns, M. Matthews, Henry Gerdel, Art Clubb, Bill Barron, Fay Pettit, Oscar Collier, Dick Weaver, and Colonel Ferguson, band president. Heald, Coffeen, and Tynan became some of the town's leading businessmen. Burns and Neely ran the printing press for the *Sheridan Post*; Gerdel was a shoemaker; Pettit painted most of the signs on buildings around town; Weaver ran the Arctic Saloon; Barron was the music instructor; Clubb became a mine manager; Collier became a jeweler; and Charles Thurmond was a carpenter. "Colonel" Ferguson copartnered with I. E. Farnham to build the Sheridan Roller Mills.

This store complex was built by Henry Coffeen in 1888 and included groceries, millinery, stationery, and dry goods. Coffeen's Hall was located on the upper floor of the larger building on the right, and rooms there were used for dances, meetings, church services, and, at times, the post office. Coffeen organized the first Sheridan College in 1898 and held classes on the second floor. C. W. Garbutt (left) came to the area with a cattle outfit from Colorado. He married John Loucks's daughter Annie May and ran the grocery store for several years before becoming postmaster. When this photograph was taken in the 1890s, Coffeen's store was headquarters for the Wells Fargo Express Office. The building lasted into the early 1920s and was replaced with the Lotus Theater that became the WYO Theater, which still stands on the site.

Henry Coffeen came to Big Horn, Wyoming, in 1884 and built a general store, started a sawmill, helped organize Big Horn's Mount Hope Cemetery, and organized Johnson County's first fair in 1885. In anticipation of the railroad's arrival, Coffeen disassembled his store and rebuilt it on Sheridan's Main Street in 1888. In 1889, Coffeen was elected to the Wyoming Constitutional Convention, where he successfully argued for women's suffrage, along with statehood in 1890. He served as Wyoming's second congressman from 1892–1894 under Pres. Grover Cleveland. About the same time, Coffeen argued the need for locating Fort Mackenzie in Sheridan, and in 1904, he was instrumental in obtaining funds for the Carnegie Library, built the following year. Henry's son Herbert opened a store called the TeePee Shop, which sold American Indian crafts and western art by Joseph Sharp and Bill Gollings.

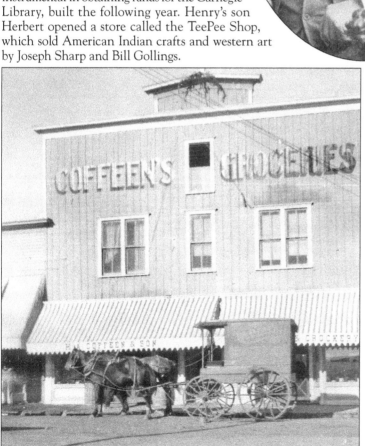

Sheridan's Bank of Commerce was founded in 1893 and occupied the false-front building at the northeast corner of Main Street and Smith Alley. In 1894, the bank moved to its impressive new quarters, which also included a distinctive angled entrance, next to the new city hall. The frame building was later used by a number of businesses, including a popular café called the Dutch Lunch.

The Congregational Church was built on the southwest corner of Main and Burkitt Streets in 1892 on what is known as Court House Hill. In 1902, it was moved to the southeast corner of Brooks and Works Streets to make way for the new county courthouse. A brick church replaced the little frame building in 1912, and the original church moved again and was used by the Second Baptist Church congregation.

The W. R. Kegerreis store was located on the west side of North Main Street, between Alger and Mandel Streets, and the Bucket of Blood Saloon was its neighbor to the south. It is typical of the early wooden frame businesses that were replaced by brick buildings during the ensuing boom that came with the railroad's arrival and opening of the coal mines.

The City Feed Yard was located at the west end of Mandel Street. Perry Hulse (center) holds one of the horses. He would later open a hardware store with George June on Main Street. Cattle, horse, and sheep feeds provided supplemental food for the stock industries in the area, as well as food for horses and milk cows kept in the city.

Looking toward the southwest side of Main Street about 1890, Coffeen's store is at the center of the photograph. To the left of Coffeen's, S. A. Leaverton's former store housed the Masonic Lodge upstairs, and the post office occupied rooms on the ground floor. To the left of Coffeen's, a barbershop, Loucks and Becker Furniture, and the Bank of Sheridan complete the block.

Looking north on Main Street in 1892, brick buildings start to appear in anticipation of the railroad's arrival. Coffeen's store complex is on the left. New brick buildings housed Forrest and Lord's Liquors, Jake Webber's Shoes, and the first structure used as the county courthouse.

The first cabin in Sheridan County was actually built in Big Horn, Sheridan's neighbor to the south. A native of Illinois, builder Oliver Perry Hanna came to the area as a member of Gen. George Crook's forces in 1876. Hanna returned in 1878 and became a successful businessman, building the Oriental Hotel and formally establishing the town of Big Horn in 1881. He later relocated to Sheridan because of the railroad.

Thomas T. Tynan was another of Sheridan's earliest movers and shakers, and can also be seen in the photograph on the front cover. Tynan came to Sheridan in 1882 as the J. H. Conrad store's bookkeeper. Tynan started Sheridan's second newspaper, the *Sheridan Enterprise*, with Fay Sommers in 1887. The *Enterprise* became northern Wyoming's first daily newspaper in 1909. The *Post* and the *Enterprise* merged in 1923, forming the *Sheridan Post-Enterprise*.

A fire at the Sheridan Brewery prompted the organization of Sheridan's fire department in 1890, and the first Fireman's Ball was held on February 14, 1890. James W. Enochs (in the white shirt) was the first chief. The band, hose cart, and engine companies posed for the photographer on July 4, 1890, in front of Morey's Blacksmith and Carriage shop on the southeast corner of Main and Brundage Streets.

Heavy snowfall in the winter of 1893–1894 prompted this photograph, which shows substantial development on the north end of Main Street. With the railroad's arrival at about the same time, this area would quickly fill with new, modern brick buildings, and a bell tower sits atop the new city hall and fire department.

Two

SHERIDAN IS NOW CONNECTED TO THE OUTSIDE WORLD!

Almost half of Sheridan's 1,000 residents gathered at the depot to welcome the first passenger train at 10:00 a.m. on November 18, 1892. Burlington and Missouri River Railroad executives had announced their intent to build the line through Sheridan as early as 1888, and this news had the most significant impact on the town's growth. Sheridan was indeed connected, and more of the world discovered Sheridan.

Edward Gillette, seen in his depot office across from the Sheridan Inn, completed the survey for the new rail route in 1890. The Burlington and Missouri Railroad went first to Gillette, named for its surveyor, before coming to Sheridan by way of Clearmont in eastern Sheridan County. Gillette made his home in Sheridan and married Henry Coffeen's daughter Hallie.

Sheridan always had the inside track on its selection as the railroad's route through northern Wyoming. Several of the Burlington and Missouri Railroad officials from Omaha owned property in the Sheridan area and realized the value of expansion there. With local investors Edward A. Whitney, Horace Alger, and C. H. Grinnell, they formed the Sheridan Land Company, which built the Sheridan Inn in 1893, right across from the B&M Depot.

Employees of the CB&Q Railroad are shown in the Sheridan roundhouse around 1910. The Burlington and Missouri River Railroad later became known as the CB&Q, for Chicago, Burlington, and Quincy, and is the forerunner of today's Burlington-Northern Santa Fe.

The railroad tracks crossed Little Goose Creek on this covered bridge south of the train yards and skirted Sheridan's warehouse district, including the Sheridan Commercial Company, the D&D Hardware warehouse, and the Merchants' Transfer, a moving and storage company. The stone building to the right was Sheridan's electric plant near the present intersection of Broadway and First Streets.

A crowd gathers around the wreck of a Burlington train in October 1904. The train lost its brakes coming down Sheridan Hill east of town and crashed into a train parked in the Burlington rail yards north of the depot. The Sheridan Inn and the Burlington depot can be seen in the background.

This 1910 photograph shows the old depot to the right of the train and the new brick depot on the left. The brick depot still stands fronting Broadway Street, a northern extension of Scott Street, one of the streets laid out in Sheridan's first 40 acres. The old wooden depot has been relocated, and both depots house businesses now.

Train No. 41 and its crew are shown on Wednesday, May 13, 1914, at the depot. Pictured from left to right are the fireman, engineer (identified as P. E. Allen), conductor, brakeman, and flagman. The railroad carried passengers as well as freight in Sheridan until 1969. Since then, only the freight service has continued, and long coal trains are frequent sights.

During the World War II years, the American Red Cross, the American Legion, and other organizations operated the Sheridan Canteen in the depot. They provided free meals, drinks, postcards, and magazines to servicemen passing through Sheridan.

The Sheridan Inn was built in 1893 by the Sheridan Land Company, which included local investors as well as Burlington and Missouri River Railroad officials. Architect Thomas Rogers Kimball's visit to a Scottish hunting lodge inspired the inn's design, which included 69 gabled windows. George and Lucy Canfield were the inn's first managers and were known for their sumptuous dinners and gracious hospitality.

Sherman Canfield, who succeeded his father, George, as inn manager, stands behind the desk in the inn's lobby, known to locals as the office. The inn featured the first running-water bathtubs and electric lights in town, and the first telephone line was connected to a downtown drugstore. Inn guests have included such notables as Ernest Hemingway, Will Rogers, Bob Hope, Robert Taylor, and several presidents.

Sheridan Inn manager George Canfield was responsible for acquiring the inn's furnishings, including the saloon's bar. The bar was made from American oak with a mahogany countertop and included the front and back bars, wine cooler, liquor cabinet, and cigar case. Although there is no maker's identification, its features are identical to those in the 1892 B. A. *Stevens Billiard and Bar Goods* catalog. Locals and tourists can still enjoy a cold one where Buffalo Bill bought rounds for the house.

George Canfield is second from the left at the 1893 New Year's Eve Ball. Lucy Canfield and George Beck led the dance. Beck originated a popular drink in the inn's saloon called the Wyoming Slug, a concoction of champagne and whiskey. Beck also built the first flour mill in Wyoming and was Buffalo Bill's partner in the Shoshone Land and Irrigation Company, which developed the town of Cody, Wyoming.

In 1894, Buffalo Bill Cody became a Sheridan Land Company partner when he purchased the Sheridan Inn's furnishings and opened the W. F. Cody Transportation Company behind the inn. George Canfield managed the operations, which included the livery barn with feed and sale stable, a stage line, freighting service, and mail carrier. The inn's mud wagon ferried passengers back and forth from town, then about a mile away.

Buffalo Bill Cody auditioned local cowboys for the Wild West show from the comfort of the inn's large porch. Some of the cowboys' wives were featured in one of the Wild West's acts. The ladies rode sidesaddle and, with their partners, performed a square dance on horseback. The inn is now operated by the Sheridan Heritage Center, and a Wild West show is held as an annual fund-raiser.

Buffalo Bill Cody's family made their first visit to the Sheridan Inn in April 1894, which was probably the occasion of this photograph. The group includes, from left to right, (first row) Winnie Grinnell (on bicycle and daughter of C. H. Grinnell), Lucy Canfield (in chair), Clara Grinnell, C. H. Grinnell, holding son Lawrence on his lap, Cody's granddaughter Clara Boal, inn proprietor George Canfield (with dog), George Beck, unidentified, and inn clerk Morgan; (second row) Rufus Rhodes (Mrs. Canfield's brother) Lucas Boyde (engineer and geologist), two unidentified people, Mrs. Bud Williams, unidentified; Horton Boal (with dark mustache), Arta Cody Boal, unidentified, Elizabeth Canfield, Buffalo Bill Cody, unidentified, Captain Palmer (Sheridan Land Company partner with hand on post), three unidentified people, Irma Cody, and Edward Gillette (hands in pocket). Shortly after this visit, Cody became part owner of the Sheridan Inn. Cody's son-in-law Horton Boal committed suicide in the inn's room 52 in 1902.

Buffalo Bill Cody, on horseback at far right, was a frequent guest at the inn through the early 1900s, including in 1905 for divorce proceedings against his wife, Louisa. Ultimately, the divorce was not granted. Development of the town of Cody, Wyoming, then took much of his time, and Cody's next visit to Sheridan was not until 1910.

Buffalo Bill Cody rode in a buggy on August 9, 1914, his last parade appearance in Sheridan. Cody's Wild West show was sold in bankruptcy in 1913 and was absorbed by the Sells-Floto Circus, which brought him back to Sheridan for the last time. Cody died on January 10, 1917, at his sister's home in Denver.

By the 1960s, the Sheridan Inn was not profitable and was almost demolished to make way for a shopping center. The Sheridan County Historical Society stepped in to raise funds to stay the wrecking ball and purchased the Buffalo Bill Bar to prevent its sale and removal. But the society could not raise sufficient funds to purchase the inn and the land it sat on. Heiress and artist Neltje Kings purchased the inn in the nick of time, remodeled it, and opened an art gallery there. The inn's restaurant operation continued in the saloon and the dining room. In the 1990s, the inn was purchased by a new non-profit organization, the Sheridan Heritage Center, who has managed it since then. At the time of this writing, the Sheridan Inn is undergoing much-needed restoration so that it can reopen as a hotel once again.

Beginning in 1893, the Tongue River Tie Flume transported railroad ties and cut lumber from the Big Horn Mountain harvest camps northeast of Sheridan to the Tongue River at the foot of the mountains. There the ties and wood floated on to the railhead in Ranchester, Wyoming, where ties were then used for railroad construction.

The flume was essentially an elevated, V-shaped canal made of several million board feet of lumber. Consisting of several branches, the flume's combined length was approximately 35 miles. High and low trestles maintained the flume's downward slope, which passed through several tunnels along the way. The longest flume in the world became quite a tourist destination, and many locals and visitors posed for photographs on or in the flume.

Lumberjacks known as "tie hacks" used broad axes to cut the ties from logs that were 11 to 18 inches in diameter and from 60 to 80 feet long. Whole logs were too large for the flume, so only ties and cut lumber were sent down and used mostly for shingles, telephone poles, and mine props. Tie hacks stopped for a photograph with William Wondra (in a white shirt) outside his saloon in the nearby town of Dayton.

Ties could reach speeds of up to 80 miles per hour on their journey down the mountain. Only a few courageous, or "thirsty," lumbermen rode long narrow boats down the flume, usually making the frightening voyage only once. Dead Man's Point was another stretch of the flume aptly named. Here the highest trestle on the system bridged a 300-foot drop over Tongue River Canyon. Four men died while building this section in 1894.

Several dams, holding ponds, worker camps, and sawmills, like the one at Woodrock shown here, supported the year-round harvest operations. A fire destroyed the Rockwood I camp in 1899, but it was rebuilt as Rockwood II camp. When milling operations shifted to another location, the new camp was named Woodrock. The flumes were used for 20 years, and about 250 men were employed in the camps.

Use of the flume ceased in 1913 because of decreased demand for ties and several unfortunate business reverses, including a suspicious fire at the Ranchester lumberyard. Local ranchers and homesteaders appropriated lumber from the flume for barns, houses, and fence posts. Flume remnants can still be seen in two tunnels and in a few remote locations. It is still a popular destination for hikers and flume enthusiasts.

Three

SHERIDAN'S TICKET TO PROSPERITY

"It's Coming!" shouted a newspaper headline in 1891. The arrival of the railroad signaled growth and prosperity. Sheridan was fortunate indeed. Sheridan's potential coal resources attracted the railroad, and timber from the Big Horn Mountains supplied the ties the railroad ran on. By the mid-1910s, many brick buildings replaced the original wooden structures, and the business district expanded by several blocks to the north and east. The boom caused by the railroad's arrival brought more businesses, more consumers, and more prosperity for the town. Trolley service started in 1911, making travel to the outskirts of town, as well as the mines, possible. In the 1910s, Sheridan's population would balloon to around 10,000, arguably exceeding that of Wyoming's capitol, Cheyenne, by about 50 residents.

Parade riders assemble in front of the Hotel Towns, built in 1896 on the site of the old Windsor Hotel, the former site of many photographs and festive occasions. A few years later, the Hotel Towns became the Great Western Hotel, and in the 1930s, a coat of stucco covered the red brick structure. The Western featured a movie-theater room, and a loudspeaker outside broadcasted the sound track up and down Main Street. Hotel accommodations ceased in the 1970s, but its downstairs retail space is still in use.

The little wooden Bank of Sheridan was replaced with this impressive brick building in 1909. It had been incorporated into the First National Bank in 1894, with many of the town's most respected businessmen and ranchers, like John B. Kendrick, the Moncreiffe brothers, and Oliver Wallop, as its new officers. The brick building was torn down in 1970 to make way for another version of the First National, and that structure still houses a bank.

A c. 1918 parade photograph allows a view of the west side of Main Street between Loucks and Brundage Streets. The First National Bank is on the left, and new brick buildings have replaced everything except Coffeen's store false fronts. Brown Drug is to the north of the bank.

George Brown serves two of Sheridan's fashion plates at the Brown Drug soda fountain in the 1890s. In 1890, Wyoming gained statehood, and Sheridan's population had increased to 281. In two more years, the railroad's arrival and the opening of the mines would make the city grow beyond John Loucks's wildest dreams.

Just past Coffeen's Hall, the new three-story Bank of Commerce was built on the southwest corner of Main and Brundage Streets in 1900. The Masonic Lodge met in the upstairs rooms until the 1950s, and the building is still in use today.

This photograph shows the rapid growth that took place from 1893 through 1911. Banks and clothing, hardware, furniture, and grocery stores opened in impressive stone and brick structures, and by 1910, Sheridan's population stood at 8,408. By 1916, Sheridan's population may have passed that of Wyoming's capitol, Cheyenne, by about 50 people.

The city hall building was only used until 1910, when the city government moved to a new structure. The 1893 city hall and fire department building was purchased by John Kendrick for $30,000 and has been used for a number of business establishments ever since. In the 1920s, the south third of the building was cut off to make way for a larger store next door.

Prior to 1893, Sheridan's city government occupied a number of different locations. The new building had rooms for the fire department equipment behind the arched doors, and the city hall offices were on the second floor. The fire bell in the large cupola summoned the volunteer fire department, seen here with its fire engine and hook-and-ladder wagon.

The Phil Sheridan No. 1 engine was built by the L Button and Sons Company of Waterford, New York, in the 1880s. It was one of the largest hand-pumped engines, called the Crane Neck No. 1. It took between 12 and 60 men to operate the engine, which could throw a stream of water at least 220 feet. The photograph shows the engine behind the fire station near the hose-drying tower.

Sporting new shirts with PSH, for Phil Sheridan Hose, the team poses before the new firehouse probably on July 4, 1893. Two men hold the brass speaking trumpets, which the foreman or chief used like a megaphone to shout instructions to the team.

The fire department readies for a parade wearing their new bib-front shirts, which identify the chief, assistant chief, and members of the Phil Sheridan Hose No. 1 and the Alert Hook and Ladder companies. John Hammond drove the team, and the horses' names were Ben and Dick.

Chief James W. Worral (in white helmet) and firemen in their new leather fire helmets stop for a picture in front of the D&D Hardware store about 1910. The store still stands at the southeast corner of Main and Brundage Streets, the site where the first photograph of the department was taken in 1890. Worral's white aluminum helmet sports a fancy brass, five-trumpet scramble, the traditional fire chief's insignia.

The Bank of Commerce was built just to the north of city hall in 1894, and its distinctive angled entry makes the building easy to identify. The southern end of a set of buildings known as the Heald Block, it shared walls with J. Frank Heald's new, elegant jewelry store, at right.

J. Frank Heald opened his first store in 1888 and was known as the pioneer jeweler. The new store, in the 100 block of North Main Street, featured stained-glass windows, and in addition to jewelry, Heald sold silver tea sets, cameras, fishing tackle, and bicycles. Heald was known for riding his high-wheeled bicycle, called a go-devil. He passed away in 1923 at the age of 63.

Forrest and Lord Liquors, above, opened in 1890 on the west side of Main Street between Brundage Street and Smith Alley. George Lord had been in the area for two years with a cattle outfit and happened upon John Loucks's platting team at work in May 1882. When Loucks informed him of the potential new town, Lord remarked, "What fools!" It seems his opinion changed after all, and he served as county sheriff for nine years and opened a hardware store with Fred C. Poll at the northwest corner of Main Street and Smith Alley, below.

Sheridan became the first city in Wyoming with a streetcar when the Sheridan Railway Company began service on August 11, 1911. Charging a nickel for most destinations, three cars ran in the city, and two cars went north to the fairgrounds and Fort Mackenzie, where passengers helped turn the trolley around on a turntable. Three Interurban cars ran to the mines. Streetcar service ended in 1924, and the Interurban to the mines lasted until 1926.

A parade passes by the Golden Rule Grocery store, Peret, Luce and Ports, a clothing store, and the Kendrick Building, which housed two furniture stores. The building with the impressive "K" emblem was later home to the Golden Rule's successor, JCPenney, which has occupied the building since 1928.

James Hill and lady clerks stand outside of the Golden Rule Grocery store on its opening day in 1908. The Golden Rule stores were franchised by James Cash Penney and several years later would become JCPenney. Penney's first Golden Rule was in Kemmerer, Wyoming.

The interior of the Golden Rule Grocery was festively decorated for its opening day in 1908. The Golden Rule expanded to John Kendrick's building in the 1920s and, by 1928, was known as the JCPenney store.

Taken about 1915, this photograph shows the east side of Main Street from Brundage to Loucks Streets. Known as D&D corner, the hardware store of Diefenderfer and Dinwiddie anchored the block. The large building in the center is the New York Store, later known as Stevens-Fryberger, which would become the largest department store in Wyoming. The building at right is the Coffeen-Ridley block, which housed five ground-floor shops with offices and apartment space above.

Ewers Grocery, located at 1 North Main Street, was in the Coffeen-Ridley Block at the northeast corner of Main and Loucks Streets. The block was constructed in 1901, and that shop in particular has been known as the PO News Stand and Café since the 1910s because of its proximity to the new post office, built around the corner on East Loucks Street. It is still a popular lunchtime destination.

Diefenderfer and Dinwiddie Hardware was built in 1902 on the southeast corner of Main and Brundage Streets, and the Elk's Lodge held their meetings in the upstairs rooms. Several restaurants have occupied the former hardware store over the years.

Perhaps because of the more impressive structures on the west side of Main Street, the east side was not as photographed. In the 1910s, the east side of Main Street still had a number of wooden buildings. D&D Hardware is to the right, and the George L. Smith Drugstore is on the northwest corner of Main and Brundage Streets. The old county courthouse building and the Cady Opera House are in the distance.

The county courthouse tower provided the vantage point for this *c.* 1918 photograph of the town. The three large buildings to the right are the Keenan Building and Apartments, the new Federal Building and Post Office (built in 1910 at a cost of $210,000) at center right, and in the distance, the new city hall.

Taken on the occasion of Pres. William Howard Taft's visit to Sheridan in October 1911, this photograph shows the new city hall, a great view of the west side of Main Street, and nearing completion on the hill, cattle baron John B. Kendrick's new home, Trail End.

Sheridan government quickly outgrew its 1893 quarters and built the new city hall at the northwest corner of Grinnell and Gould Streets in 1910. City offices and the fire department moved in the following year, and both structures are still in use. The fire bell from the 1893 building adorns the front of the 1910 city hall as a historical marker.

Sheridan's original county government offices were at the southeast corner of Main and Grinnell Streets in a large brick building constructed by Sheridan Brewery partner Peter Demple. The county government moved into its new quarters in 1904, and a building annex was added in the 1980s.

John D. Loucks opened the first library upstairs in his store and home in 1883, and the reading room served Sheridan's residents for about 10 years. Built with funds raised by the community and matched by Andrew Carnegie, the new Carnegie Library (shown here) opened in August 1905 on the northeast corner of Loucks and Brooks Streets. The Carnegie Library was replaced by a new library in 1974 and torn down to make way for a parking lot.

Owned by the state, the Wyoming General Hospital opened its doors on July 1, 1905, with beds for 45 patients. The Saberton Street facility also included quarters for the first graduating class of nurses in 1907. Deeded to the county in 1921, it housed the Sheridan County Memorial Hospital until 1954. The old hospital building served as the temporary quarters for the Northern Wyoming Community College while the campus now known as Sheridan College was under construction.

The first Baptist services were held in the old Central School, and Rev. G. W. Benton of Big Horn was the first pastor. The Baptists were one of the first congregations to organize, and they built the frame church shown here in 1889. Other churches that organized in the 1880s and 1890s include the First Congregational Church in 1884, the First Methodist Episcopal in 1888, the First Presbyterian in 1892, Holy Name Catholic Church in 1885, and St. Peter's Episcopal Church in 1893.

The Baptists quickly outgrew the little frame church and built the $15,000 brick structure shown here in 1909. The frame building was purchased by the African Methodist Episcopal Church, moved to another location, and served that congregation until the 1960s. Other large congregations moved to brick churches in the 1910s and 1920s.

By 1889, the Sheridan Brewery had expanded its operations, producing several million barrels of beer before Prohibition took affect in 1920. New products like a near beer called Sherex and several fruit-flavored soft drinks kept the brewery in business. At the end of Prohibition in 1933, brewing capacity tripled to about 600 barrels of beer a day. By 1954, the brewery produced 60,000 barrels a year, but at that same time, the Sheridan Brewery ceased its beer operation to concentrate on soda pop.

Because it has been privately owned since 1987, the John S. Taylor (elementary) School is the only one of Sheridan's schools built in the 1910s and 1920s left. Sheridan's high school, built in 1926 and later used as the Sheridan Junior High School, was torn down in 2004. An etched window at the Taylor school encouraged students with the motto, "Enter Here To Learn, Go Forth To Serve."

Four

FORTUNES MADE, HEARTS BROKEN

Rough cabins marked the site of Bald Mountain City where, in 1891, the New York City–based Fortunatus Mining Company began efforts to take gold from the Big Horns. An amalgamator—a large machine designed to absorb gold in mercury then heat the amalgam to recover the gold—was put into use in 1893. The amalgamator never recovered enough gold to make the operation pay, and Fortunatus went into receivership in 1895. Local residents formed the Bald Mountain Mining Company to take over the work, but that also failed. An attempt was made in 1931 to extract gold using cyanide. It also failed, and the gold on Bald Mountain has since remained undisturbed.

Placer miners seek gold in the Big Horn Mountains in this photograph taken some time in the 1890s. Riches, including gold and even diamonds, are known to exist in the Big Horns. But nature played a cruel joke on would-be miners in Sheridan County. The bulk of Bald Mountain's riches was in "flour gold," microscopically tiny particles that floated on water. The cost of recovering such precious minerals has always outweighed the value of the materials extracted.

Taken around 1926, this photograph shows the remains of the Bald Mountain City Hotel. It was one of the amenities at the little gold mine community that became known as the City of Broken Hearts. Other buildings included a saloon, a blacksmith shop, and a dining hall. The mine was about 62 miles northeast of Sheridan in the Big Horn Mountains above Dayton.

A more successful mining operation began in the 1890s when the arrival of coal-burning trains created a commercial use for Sheridan County's coal. William Frederick Wondra (second from right) and fellow miners stop for a photograph inside the Monarch Mine in the early 1900s. The Monarch Mine and the nearby Monarch community were opened in 1903 by Stewart Kennedy. Most of the area mines were located approximately 4 to 10 miles north of Sheridan.

Miners, horses, and a woman pose for a photograph at the Monarch Mine entrance after its opening in 1903. William Wondra (kneeling in front) wrote that "the woman was Italian, and she carried tools for her husband on top of her head." Wondra also noted "that the horses stayed in the mine all the time. They pulled the coal cars to a cable, the cable then pulled the coal out of the mine and up the tipple."

A group of Sheridan businessmen formed the Sheridan Fuel Company in 1893 and opened the first mine at Higby—later renamed Dietz—4 miles north of the city of Sheridan. The coal companies built towns with housing and amenities for the miners and their families. Dietz eventually included eight mines, the last of which closed in 1922. By then, the Sheridan Fuel Company had opened other mines that were more profitable than the Dietz operations.

The Carney Coal Company opened its Carneyville Mine in 1904. The town boasted a plentiful water supply, fire protection, public baths for the men, a large general store, a meat market, and good public schools. By 1921, the Chicago-based Peabody Coal Company had acquired Carney along with several other mines in Sheridan County's Tongue River Valley. On January 13, 1921, Peabody announced the Carneyville Mine would henceforth be named Kleenburn to reflect the company's promotion of the mine as a source of clean-burning coal.

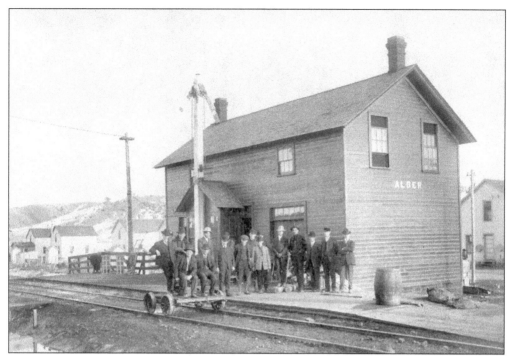

The CB&Q Railroad's Kleenburn depot was actually located closer to the town of Monarch than the Kleenburn Mine and was originally called Alger for Sheridan investor Horace Alger. Most of the mine towns had their own schools, churches, clubs, bands, and other amenities. The nearby Acme Mine maintained an underground stable for its horses and mules, and also boasted an underground banquet hall.

Amenities in Kooi included the pool hall shown in the foreground. Peter Kooi opened the mine there in July 1906. By 1912, the mine was producing 161,700 tons of coal a year. The boom times did not last. By the 1920s, Americans were converting to other fuels, and the need for coal dwindled. Kooi's mine closed in 1922, but a few families continued to live in the community.

William Wondra stands with another miner and a punching machine. Wondra wrote that the machine undermined the coal before blasting. The punching machine was later replaced by the cutting machine, similar to a chain saw, with a 9-foot-long cutter bar. By 1908, the Monarch Mine employed 450 workers with a monthly payroll of $30,000, and the town of Monarch housed a population estimated at 1,000, with 168 dwellings.

Cars loaded with coal sit on the bridge over the Tongue River. William Wondra wrote that the cars were all loaded by hand and that each car contained two to three tons of coal each. By 1913, the Monarch Mine yielded 2,500 to 3,000 tons of coal per day. Many of the Polish miners came from three Polish villages, Istebna, Koniakow, and Jaworzynka, all located near Poland's southern border with Slovakia.

This Monarch Mine entrance was called Old 70. William Wondra is seen here driving the motor so that families could tour the mine. The black man in the foreground was the chef, and the event celebrated the first load of coal brought out by the locomotive. One battery-powered locomotive replaced eight horses and could pull 400 tons of coal a day. Wondra later opened a saloon in Dayton.

William Wondra noted that the track on the left "is where the loaded cars went up, pulled by a large chain with hooks called dog chains. The track at right was for empty cars to return. At the top of the tipple, the coal is screened and dumped into railroad cars. To the right is Monarch's power house."

The Tongue River Trading Company was the official company store for the Sheridan-Wyoming Coal Company, owner of the Monarch Mine. Most of the Tongue River coal mines closed in the 1920s and 1930s—victims of the decreasing demand for coal. The Monarch Mine survived into the 1940s when the war renewed demand for coal worldwide. In the 1950s, strip mines replaced underground mining, and the Sheridan-Wyoming Coal Company closed the Monarch Mine in 1953.

Mule drivers, such as the men in this undated photograph, came not only from Sheridan, but also from around the world. Emigrants from across Europe—including England, Wales, Germany, Austria, Poland, Italy, and other Eastern European countries—flocked to Sheridan County to work the mines. At the Acme Mine, Japanese and Italian emigrant miners lived in areas called "Japtown" and "Macaroni Flats." Many of their descendants still live in Sheridan County, contributing to the area's rich cultural heritage.

The mine is unidentified, but the scene is typical for any of the mines that operated in the area. Even though motors like the one here helped transport coal quicker, the work was backbreaking, the hours long, and the men daily risked death by fire, explosions, cave-ins or, eventually, the long, lingering death of black lung disease caused by prolonged exposure to coal dust.

Advances in mining technology ultimately led to unemployment as machines replaced horses, then men. These electric drilling machines brought power and light with them and did not rely on tracks.

Surface-mining operations—also called strip-mining—replaced underground mines in the 1950s. The Sheridan-Wyoming Coal Company entered into a joint surface-mining venture with Big Horn Coal, which commenced operations near the old Acme town site. Draglines and coal haulers that could carry 20 tons required fewer operators. A revival of interest in low-sulphur coal in the 1970s brought new life into Big Horn Coal's operations, starting another coal boom and fueling Sheridan County's economy into the mid-1980s.

In coal mining, as with gold, nature dealt Sheridan County a bad hand. The coal is present in abundance, but the overburden—the amount of earth that must be stripped away to get to the underlying coal beds—measures in hundreds of feet, making surfacing-mining a costly operation. Big Horn Coal's loss was a major blow to Sheridan County's energy-dependent economy, and the county went through an economic depression. In the late 1990s, the extraction of coal-bed methane began another energy boom in the area.

Five

REAL COWBOYS
AND INDIANS

Stockmen moved into the area that would soon be Sheridan just after the resolution of American Indian conflicts in the late 1870s. South of Sheridan, cattlemen gathered for this photograph taken near Big Horn around 1894. Pictured from left to right are W. H. "Doc" Spear, Bill Glasgow, Andy Martinson, Lew Burgess, Nelson Darlington, Guy Wood, unidentified, William Eckerson, Aaron Darlington, Will Schneider, and Bill Leavitt. One of the largest and earliest ranches in the area was started to the west of Sheridan by brothers Matt and Al Patrick, who also had the stage line contract from Rock Creek in southern Wyoming to Custer Station on the Yellowstone River. The PK Ranch is still one of the largest in the area, and portions of it have been set aside as a nature conservancy.

Sheridan's Fifth Street was once one of the area's major stock trails, as well as the emigrant route of the Bozeman Trail. Although cattle are hauled in trailers now, Eaton's, a dude ranch, still runs its horse herd up Fifth Street to its ranch at Wolf, Wyoming, every spring. Another early ranch was the O 4 Bar west of Ranchester, established by Samuel H. Hardin in 1880.

C. H. Grinnell and his cousin George W. Holdrege, the general manager of the Burlington and Missouri River Railroad, established the Wrench Ranch, also one of the area's earliest, in 1880. The ranch's brand looks like a curved, double-ended wrench. In 1946, John and Ruth Rice (pictured here) bought the ranch for their polled Hereford operation. The Rices sold the ranch in 1995 to the present owner, Neltje Kings.

One of Sheridan's best-known cattle barons was John B. Kendrick (above with his son Manville). Kendrick trailed cattle from Texas to Wyoming in 1879 and acquired his own herds. Headquartered at the OW Ranch, the Kendrick Cattle Company's operation eventually grew to 200,000 acres on 10 properties in Wyoming and Montana. In 1908, Kendrick built a town home for his wife, Eula, and their children Rosa May and Manville. The Flemish Revival–styled mansion (below) was finished in 1913, but Kendrick spent little time at the home he named Trail End. Kendrick was elected state senator, governor, and U.S. senator. One of Sheridan's earliest benefactors, Kendrick donated 35 acres for Pioneer Park and 600 acres for the Kendrick Municipal Golf Course. Kendrick's home is now the Trail End State Historic Site, Wyoming's premier historic house museum.

On the heels of ranching came a uniquely western phenomenon—the dude ranch—as ranchers discovered that not only friends, but also complete strangers were willing to pay for the privilege of riding horses and even helping with chores. In 1890, Daniel T. Hilman operated the first dude ranch in Sheridan County near Big Horn when he accepted two summer guests—the first of a long string of visitors.

Dude ranches flourished in Sheridan County in the early half of the 19th century. The Dude Ranchers' Association in the West was formed in 1926 to set standards for the industry, as well as to attract visitors. The Burlington Railroad helped out by printing special maps of dude ranches in Wyoming and Montana. Postcards like the one above featured dudes and dudines (female dudes) at play.

The Eaton brothers, Howard, Willis Larimer, and Alden Eaton, launched the nation's first dude ranch in the 1880s at their ranch in North Dakota at the suggestion of friends from back east who enjoyed the Eatons' hospitality. The brothers moved their ranch to Wolf, just north of Sheridan, in 1903—the second dude ranch in Sheridan County. The ranch remains one of the better-known dude operations and has been popular with Hollywood filmmakers as well. Below, Eaton's bedroll wagons are shown leading a party of dudes to Yellowstone Park in 1908.

Willis M. Spear operated the Spear-O-Wigwam Ranch from 1923 to 1945 in the Big Horn Mountains southwest of Sheridan. Spear represented Sheridan County in Wyoming's state senate for 12 years and was the father of noted Sheridan County photographer and historian Elsa Spear Byron, shown here with four of her daughters.

Tepee Lodge was located in the Big Horn Mountains 22 miles southwest of Sheridan and was run by the Allen Fordyce family from 1929 through 1947. With the stock market crash of 1929 and the ensuing Depression, travel to ranches in the West was more attractive to those who could no longer afford to tour Europe.

Dudes and dudines relax at one of TePee's rustic cabins. Real cowboy wranglers taught dudes how to ride, rope, and sing cowboy songs. The dude ranches employed many local cowboys, waitresses, housekeepers, cattle, and lots of horses.

In a photograph that looks like a scene from a Roy Rogers movie, newly arrived dudes are serenaded by a cowboy guitarist on the porch of their TePee cabin. Quite a few dudes enjoyed their western experience so much that they returned to the area and purchased their own ranches over the years, bringing both eastern money and influence that has benefited the area.

Most visitors to the area are surprised to learn that the sport of polo is alive and well in Sheridan County. While not a typical western sport, this sport of kings found a western home, introduced by three Britons in the 1890s. The Moncreiffe brothers bought a ranch just outside Big Horn, named it the Quarter Circle A, and built the house shown below. Malcolm Moncreiffe and Oliver Henry Wallop, above, seated in front, and Malcolm's brother William, above, standing at left, partnered to provide 22,550 remounts for the British cavalry engaged in South Africa's Boer War in the mid-1890s. The Moncreiffes became known for the quality of their stock, including horses, polo ponies, Hereford cattle, and prize-winning sheep. William Moncreiffe's registered brand is the second oldest in the state of Wyoming.

William Moncreiffe married in 1908, and his family remained on the ranch until 1923 when it was sold to Bradford Brinton, shown here with the Sheridan Inn's mud wagon. Brinton, an Illinois businessman, vacationed at the ranch, collected western art, and enlarged the home. After his death in 1936, his sister Helen established the trust, now known as the Bradford Brinton Memorial and Museum, which showcases the historic home and an art gallery.

Malcolm Moncreiffe, standing between his wife, Amy (left), and Charlotte Walsh, was the driving force behind polo in Sheridan County. In 1901, Malcolm developed the first polo field on what would become the Polo Ranch southwest of Big Horn, where polo was played until 1984. Since then, the game has been played at the Big Horn Equestrian/Events Center, where world-class players and horses appear each summer.

The second son of the fifth earl of Portsmouth, Oliver Henry Wallop came to America in 1883. He settled first in Miles City, Montana, before coming to Big Horn in 1891 and eventually purchasing the Canyon Ranch, shown below. He and Malcolm Moncreiffe, along with other British stockmen, were involved with polo in the Otter Creek, Montana, area before coming to Big Horn. Wallop's wife, Marguerite, and Amy Moncreiffe were sisters. Wallop became an American citizen in 1904 and was elected to the Wyoming legislature in 1908. The death of his older brother in 1925 forced him to assume the earlship and membership in the British House of Lords. His grandson, Malcolm Wallop, served for many years as one of Wyoming's U.S. senators.

In addition to Big Horn's Polo Ranch (shown here), the game was played at several sites around Sheridan as early as 1897. Cowboys played polo around Saberton Avenue before the hospital was built there and at Sheridan's original fairgrounds south of town. In 1900, the first match played for a cup took place behind the old Western Hotel near Works and Brooks Streets.

The local Big Horn team, called the Magpies, wore distinctive black-and-white vests. They traveled to Denver, Colorado Springs, and Glenwood, Colorado, to compete in matches with teams, including several fielded by the U.S. Army. Pictured from left to right are Lee Bullington, John Cover, Malcolm Moncreiffe, and Robert Walsh as they prepare for a match with the 12th Cavalry team in 1907 or 1908.

Agricultural pursuits led to fairs as farmers and ranchers gathered to show off their prize stock—such as the prize horses at the first fair in Big Horn, then Johnson County in September 1885. Horse racing and harness racing were among the activities. It would be three years before Sheridan County split off from its parent and another five years before the Wyoming Territory would become a state.

Spectators gather in the 1890s to watch an event at the original fairgrounds south of the original Sheridan town site on what is now Coffeen Avenue. The racetrack built there could still be seen in aerial photographs as late as the 1960s. Coffeen Avenue today is part of the state highway system and is known as the busiest street in Wyoming.

A cowboy hangs tight on a bronc in the photograph above, taken during an event at Sheridan's original fairgrounds. "Rodeo" wasn't yet part of the vocabulary, but riding rough stock was all in a day's work for cowhands, and they did not mind showing their skills in competition. Below are the Sheridan County Fairgrounds located off Fifth Street, which was purchased for horse racing in 1906 by the Sheridan County Fair Association. By 1919, the fair association had apparently fallen on hard times. According to newspapers of the times, Sheridan County acquired the fairgrounds site that year for $8,000.

The "warbonnet race" was a popular event at the Sheridan County Fairgrounds. American Indians, especially Crow from the nearby reservation in southern Montana, have a long history of involvement with Sheridan County horse events. In the photograph below, Crow women were the jockeys. Today the World Championship Indian Relay races take place at the beginning of each day of the Sheridan-WYO Rodeo and are some of the most thrilling and popular events. American Indian jockeys ride three different horses in a relay around the arena track. Their teammates hold the waiting horses, who start running before their jockey dismounts the previous horse. The jockey's creative and skillful transfer to the new horse, all done without the aid of a saddle, creates the most excitement, along with the dash to the finish.

One of the earliest shows in the city of Sheridan was the three-day "Indian and Pioneer Stampede" in 1914. Organized by Dr. William Frackleton, an area promoter, pioneer dentist, and author, the event featured broncs, steer roping, a 25-mile automobile race, polo, a stagecoach holdup, and a number of events featuring American Indians—complete with a Crow tepee village.

Rodeos have a long tradition in Sheridan County, and an Old Time Cow-Boys Reunion was held at Dayton, Wyoming, on July 4, 1896. It featured bucking broncos and tying-down steers. Above, spectators watch the PK Ranch rodeo in 1929. The PK ranch, west of Sheridan on Soldier Creek,

From the beginning, the Sheridan-WYO Rodeo included a strong American Indian presence, as evidenced by this photograph of the first Sheridan-WYO Rodeo parade in 1931. The goal of the rodeo was three-fold: to keep Sheridan residents home, to provide a mid-summer event in Sheridan, and to advertise Sheridan to tourists. From the start, the rodeo attracted some of the biggest names in the sport of its day.

featured a natural amphitheater and hosted rodeos in 1928 and 1929. The success of those ventures contributed to the organization of the Sheridan-WYO Rodeo in 1931.

The Sheridan-WYO Rodeo was suspended in 1942 and 1943, a casualty of World War II. When it returned in 1944, it was more of a local rodeo for working cowboys. Through 1950, it was called the Bots Sots Stampede. This 1949 rodeo parade photograph was taken by Rochford Studios in Sheridan. Bot Sots is a Crow phrase meaning "the very best."

Part of the rodeo pageantry was the annual selection of a rodeo queen. In 1952, Lucy Yellowmule, a shy Crow girl, was selected for the honor by popular vote. Aided by reporter Howard Sinclair, Lucy turned her reign into an opportunity to improve American Indian and white relations, which had become strained over the years. She and her court, shown below with William Henry Harrison, his wife Betty, and Sinclair (right), made many public appearances to dispel myths and share American Indian culture. Gradually, new appreciation was gained on both sides. Sheridan earned several national awards that recognized the improvements, and Lucy traveled to Washington, D.C., to accept them on Sheridan's behalf. Capitalizing on Lucy's success, white and American Indian leaders organized an event called All-American Indian Days, which celebrated all tribal cultures and featured an annual pageant to select Miss Indian America.

Six

GETTING ALONG
WITH THE
NEIGHBORS

In the 1890s, Sheridanites began observing and commemorating the anniversaries of historic Indian Wars events. As early as 1897, a special excursion train shuttled folks back and forth from Sheridan to the Custer battlefield (seen here) and to the Crow Agency, about 60 miles north of Sheridan. The Crow had allied with Generals Custer and Crook during the conflicts of 1876, and they celebrated as well. These commemorations began the reconciliation process, capitalized on the area's history, including one of the greatest American Indian festivals of all time, and helped neighbors find some common ground.

In 1908, Col. Henry Carrington, his wife Frances, and several members of his command returned to Sheridan to visit the site of old Fort Phil Kearny, the post the colonel built in 1866. Pictured here from left to right are (first row) Jack Owens, William Murphy, J. Newcomer, Sgt. Sam Gibson, and S. S. Peters; (second row) William Daley, General Freeman, Carrington (in uniform), John Owens, Frances Carrington, Mrs. Freeman, Mrs. Strawn, J. Strawn, and Dennis Driscoll.

The group stopped for a photograph at the site of the fort's old flagpole. The army abandoned the post in 1868, and Red Cloud's warriors burned it later that year. Fort Phil Kearny had been one of three posts built to offer protection to Bozeman Trail travelers on their way to Montana's goldfields, and it is about 30 miles south of Sheridan.

The party commemorated the event with the unveiling of a monument to the members of Col. Carrington's command killed on December 21, 1866, in an encounter with Sioux and Cheyenne warriors under Red Cloud and a young Crazy Horse that has become known as the Fetterman Massacre.

Col. Carrington's second wife, Frances (at Carrington's left), accompanied him on the trip. She had arrived at the fort as the wife of Lt. George Grummond, Captain Fetterman's cavalry detachment commander, and left his widow when Carrington's command evacuated the post later that month. Now the Fort Phil Kearny State Historic Site, the visitor's center, and the partially reconstructed stockade help tell the story. Much of the fort's historic view shed has also been preserved.

One of the largest commemorations was held in 1902, and Dr. William Frackelton and first settler O. P. Hanna were the event's organizers. Serving dental patients on the Crow Reservation as well as in Sheridan, Frackelton was in a unique position to direct the Mid-Summer Carnival, which featured a sham battle. This was probably the first reenactment of the Battle of the Little Bighorn staged by a western town.

In an ironic twist, the Crow, led by Chief Medicine Crow (at center with the U.S. flag), were persuaded to play the role of their Sioux and Cheyenne enemies in the mock battle, and they assumed their roles with great enthusiasm. Members of the Wyoming National Guard would portray Custer's troops and were reluctantly resigned to defeat.

The Sheridan Post.

SHERIDAN, WYOMING, THURSDAY, JUNE 26, 1902. PRICE, 5 CENTS

1902 MID SUMMER CARNIVAL

JULY 3, 4, 5.
SHERIDAN, WYOMING.

INDIANS, COWBOYS, HOT TIME.

...EVERYBODY COME...

This is the opportunity for all North Wyoming to make

The Great Gala Day of the Northwest

In The Land of Sunshine and Promise

Iowa's Best Band	Rough Riders
27 Gold Medal Artists	Races Polo
St. Xavier Mission Band	War Dances Etc.
18 Indian Boys	

1000 Indians in Native Costumes in Daily Parade

Grand Reproduction of the CUSTER BATTLE, With Government and State Troops and the Scouts and War Chiefs who were near the Scene of that Eventful Tragedy.

Low Rates on The Burlington From All Points

WM. FRACKELTON, MANAGER

There was something for everyone at the Mid-Summer Carnival. Sheridan touted its proximity to the local Crow Reservation and promised thrills akin to those made popular by Buffalo Bill's Wild West show. Organizers had attempted the Custer reenactment in 1900, but the carnival went on without the sham battle.

Participants and spectators gathered in front of the Sheridan Inn, and a 16-piece band of American Indian boys from the Xavier Mission provided entertainment. In cooperation with the Burlington and Missouri River Railroad, special excursion trains brought scores of tourists, and an estimated 10,000 visitors witnessed the events. The railroad sent its photographer, Louis R. Bostwick, to record the events, and famed western artist Charles Schreyvogel sketched scenes like a wartime correspondent.

The parade left the Sheridan Inn and proceeded south on Main Street, passing under a commemorative arch at the intersection of Main and Brundage Streets. The arch was made of fabric stretched over a wooden framework and included painted details and electric lights. The Bank of Commerce's new building and Coffeen's Store can be seen in the background.

On successive days of the three-day festival, the parade went up and down Main Street, stopping every block for impromptu war dances. On the Fourth of July, the parade led the crowd to Coffeen's Grove, a hilly area on the banks of Little Goose Creek where the sham battle began at about 4:30 p.m.

Posters advertised 1,000 American Indians in native costumes in the daily parades, and guests of honor were surely the Crow veterans of the 1876 campaigns, including three who had served as Custer's scouts: White-Man-Runs-Him, Hairy Moccasin, and Curley, the only survivor of Custer's immediate command. Shown here are American Indian participants posed in the middle of Main Street.

Even young Crow girls were dressed in their finery. Local businessman George Messick captured this image of Margaret Yellow Crane and Iron Horse in front of the City Hall Fire House and the Bank of Commerce.

During one of the parades, Sheridan merchant George Messick snapped this photograph of Crow participants at the northeast corner of Main and Loucks Streets, later the site of the P.O. News Stand.

Masks were apparently part of the costume for one of the spectacles was described in Sheridan newspapers as "the Hideous Parade," and George Messick captured the "most picturesque and hideous costumes," which delighted eastern visitors and promised to "represent the Indians in the most realistic way."

Many citizens snapped photographs of these parades, and this image of the same masked participants was taken by Virginia Belle Spear, the mother of famous area photographer and historian Elsa Spear Byron.

Well dressed for the occasion, Crow warrior Flower was one of the most photographed participants and signaled the start of the battle. Chief Medicine Crow and Bear Claw led 200 Crow warriors, and Maj. C. Z. Zander led 96 men of Companies A, D, and G of the Wyoming National Guard.

Spectators on the hillsides near Canby and Park Streets knew the story of the actual battle, but the reenactment took a slightly different turn behind the scenes, according to the account in Dr. William Frackelton's book *Sagebrush Dentist*. (Photograph courtesy Denver Public Library, Western History Collection, Louis R. Bostwick, photographer, Call Number X-33948.)

Maj. C. Z. Zander informed Dr. William Frackelton that the troopers would not allow the colors to be taken. Dr. Frackelton, who had been invited to ride as an American Indian, told Chief Medicine Crow that Custer's troops had reacted the same way and that he (Frackelton) would ensure that the Crow would end up with the flag. The battle proceeded normally with the heroic but systematic "killing" of Custer's troops.

When it came time for the final scene, Dr. William Frackelton galloped into the "last stand" contingent and seized the flag. This was not in the script. Stunned, a furious Major Zander refused to die, challenged Frackelton with a few choice words, ripped off the blond wig he was wearing, and hurled it at the dentist. Frackelton deftly caught the golden "scalp" and waved it high in the air, signifying the American Indian's victorious end to the battle once again. (Photograph courtesy Denver Public Library, Western History Collection, Louis R. Bostwick, photographer, Call Number X-33956.)

Following in Lucy Yellowmule's steps, Arlene Wesley of the Yakima tribe was crowned the first Miss Indian America in 1953. Miss Indian America reigned as queen for one year and served as a goodwill ambassador, sharing American Indian culture and dispelling myths. Young women from all over the country and from many different tribes and circumstances competed. (Photograph by Don Diers.)

The selection of Lucy Yellowmule as the 1952 rodeo queen was the impetus for an event that did much to foster good relations with Sheridan's American Indian neighbors. In 1953, Howard Sinclair, Don Diers, and other Sheridan business leaders and their local Crow counterparts founded a pageant and American Indian expo called All-American Indian Days, which featured an annual pageant for the title of Miss Indian America.

Impressive parades were a feature of All-American Indian Days where the contestants could display their elaborate costumes. Even the horses were highly decorated. American Indian church services, crafts, and foods were part of the festivities, and an Outstanding Indian was chosen for his or her contributions each year. (Photograph by Don Diers.)

The pageant was held at the Sheridan County Fairgrounds where dancing, music, horse races, and American Indian crafts were featured. Visitors mixed freely with the American Indian participants in the Indian village, and much goodwill and friendship was the result. The contestants and the reigning Miss Indian America lived with host families in Sheridan, and this led to many lifelong friendships. Miss Indian America traveled across the country and, in some cases, to Europe. For many of the women, it was their first trip in a train or airplane.

Miss Indian America V was Gros Ventre Ruth Larson. Because of the enormous effort to put on the festivities, the pageant moved to Bismark, North Dakota, and was held there until 1989. Possibly due to the enormous cost to host the pageant, it was discontinued that year. In the meantime, many tribes had begun to hold their own powwows and fairs.

Seven

THROUGH FIRE, FLOOD, AND THE TEST OF TIME

Although the Commercial was not the first store in Sheridan, it has certainly outlasted all the others, surviving the fire engulfing the building in this 1915 photograph. Organized in 1892 as the Sheridan County Commercial Company, the company marked its 115th year in business in 2007. Founder J. Dana Adams headed the company, and many other early and prominent Sheridan businessmen were the first stockholders. It weathered the flood of 1923 and, more recently, the economic threat of national chain stores. The Commercial has the distinction of being Sheridan's oldest establishment still doing business at the same location.

Most western towns boasted their own opera houses, and Sheridan was no exception. In fact, it had two. The Cady Opera House was built in 1893 and occupied the third floor of the impressive Cady Building on the northeast corner of Main and Alger Streets. Opera in the late 19th century was as common a form of entertainment, as movies are today, and touring troupes of singers performed operatic selections as well as the popular songs of the day.

While few performances were classified as operas in the classical sense, the house provided a venue for the performing arts, including local and touring vocal and instrumental music groups, musical theater, plays, melodramas, and vaudeville. The Cady's ground floor housed a grocery store, and local businesses and county government occupied the second floor for a time. The Elks Lodge met at the Cady before its new quarters were built in 1902.

The Cady quickly became Sheridan's cultural center, hosting elegant affairs as well as popular community productions and a musical revue presented by the Sheridan Cornet Band in 1899. Ironically, the Cady Opera House caught fire in the early morning hours of October 7, 1906, after the performance of a touring play called *The Runaway Match*. Most of the building was gutted by the fire.

John D. Helvey bought the structure in 1907 and rebuilt it, minus the third floor. For a number of years, it was known as the Helvey Hotel, but the original name was restored by a subsequent owner in 1984. The building was purchased by Pinnacle Gas Resources, Inc., for offices in 2005, and the ground floor continues to be used for retail and restaurant space. (Photograph by Archie Nash.)

Another devastating fire affected one of Sheridan's longtime businesses, the Sheridan County Commercial Company. The Commercial's first storefront was in a building erected by Edward A. Whitney in 1887 just north of the present store building on Broadway Street, a continuation of Sheridan's original Scott Street. Pictured above from left to right are William Miller, company president J. Dana Adams, A. D. Zander, and Sam Inglefield as they stand in front of the store, and the words Produce Exchange in faint lettering can be seen on the false front. In the 1902 photograph below, the old store can be seen north of the new two-story addition, which expanded to the south all the way to the corner of Alger Street.

This expansion took a few years, but by 1905, the building housed a rooming house and restaurant, butcher shop, grocery store, and a full-service hardware department that stocked clothing, feed and seed, harnesses, gas engines, farm implements, and a newfangled invention, the automobile. By the 1910 photograph above, a new facade and a balcony had been extended across the front of the old side, and the upper story of the new side had been completed. The Commercial's livery barn was a separate structure and stood to the rear of the store at the end of Alger Street. Below, the Commercial's founder, J. Dana Adams (with white beard), and his wife, Dora, visited the farm implement department. Despite, or perhaps because of the Commercial's expansion, by 1902, the company was losing money and on the verge of closing its doors.

The directors hired a young salesman by the name of Ellsworth Gwinn (left) at $75 a month whose unfortunate task was to close out the business as cheaply as possible. Gwinn quickly turned the business around and, instead of closing the store, put its ledgers back in the black. When Gwinn asked for a vacation and a raise of $75 a month, he was politely let go. In 1911, the Commercial was failing again, and Gwinn was asked to come back to bail out the company one more time. This time though, his salary was tripled, and after J. Dana Adams died in 1912, Gwinn was promoted to store manager. Ellsworth Gwinn worked his commercial magic once again, and as a result, the business flourished, and the Gwinn family name became synonymous with the Sheridan Commercial Company.

Photographs of the impressive store appeared in a publication called *Pictorial Sheridan*, a booklet designed to tout Sheridan and to attract new business, citizens, and investors. The Commercial, as it was known, was one of the most impressive stores in town, and its wide selection of merchandise provided something for any taste or pocketbook. Below, James Hill (wearing the vest) and coworkers man the grocery department. The Commercial had an ingenious system for handling cash and change. Each station had a mechanical system that transferred the cash tendered to the cash-handling department at the rear of the store. Change was made there and sent back to the original site of purchase to be returned to the customer. Department employees did not have to make change or be responsible for a cash drawer.

Sheridan Commercial Company clerks James Hill (at left, standing) and an unidentified coworker appear in several of these photographs. The black sleeve protectors were commonly worn by shopkeepers to extend the wear life of their white shirts. In the photograph below, the pair from the grocery department visits the butcher shop, which was in the southeast corner of the building. The younger man can be seen using the wall telephone.

Despite the fact that the Commercial was safely in the hands of Ellsworth Gwinn, a fire broke out about mid-morning on June 4, 1915, and by noon of the same day, the building had been reduced to a smoldering pile of wood and metal. Luckily, there were no fatalities and just one injury when a boarder from the upstairs rooming house jumped out of a second-story window to escape the flames. However, the building was a total loss, and a great deal of merchandise burned as well. No definite cause of the fire was determined, but it was thought that a spark had ignited a mouse or rat's nest in the hardware department. Below, spectators helped remove some of the merchandise, and it quickly piled up in front of the building.

Spectators watch as smoke pours from the building (left). The *Sheridan Post* reported, "It was one of the most spectacular daytime fires that ever occurred in Sheridan and was witnessed by thousands of people who crowded the street in all directions. Luckily there was but a slight breeze, else several other buildings in the wholesale district might have gone with the Commercial." As it was, the J. W. Denio Milling Company mill and elevators (below), just across the alley, had a narrow escape. At one time, the window casings of the mill were blazing, and the roof was smoking in the heat. At that juncture, a charge of dynamite was exploded under the southwest corner of the Commercial Building and helped to bring down the walls so that the danger to the mill was lessened.

Above, men viewing the ruins of the Sheridan County Commercial Company appear to be standing on a cloud of smoke but are really standing on top of the Denio Mill. With the building and merchandise losses estimated at about $53,000, it looked like another closure was inevitable. However, the store hardly skipped a beat. Ellsworth Gwinn went about rebuilding the business yet again, and in 1916, the word "County" was dropped from the company name, and new stockholders were added to the list. John B. Kendrick built the new store, which opened in 1917 at the same location, this time with the letter K for Kendrick carved in limestone on the impressive new facade. Gwinn's son George took over the store in 1942, and in 1992, the store was purchased by the Smith family, who still operate the business.

Photographs above and below show the aftermath of the 1923 downpour considered the worst flood in Sheridan's history. More than six inches of rain fell between September 27 and 30. Forty inches of rapidly melting snow in the Big Horn Mountains turned Big and Little Goose Creeks into raging torrents. Water ran a foot deep through the city. Basements were flooded; telephone lines were down; and streetlights went out. Floodwaters swept away the wooden paving blocks from downtown streets, along with several of Sheridan County's roads and bridges. Many of the paving blocks were collected for firewood. City officials warned that anyone "wrongfully appropriating paving blocks in any manner will be prosecuted." The wooden paving blocks were replaced by asphalt the following year. The Kelly tire store at right, below, was originally the Cow Boy Saloon. (Photographs by the Cox Art Shop.)

Eight

SHERIDAN'S COLORFUL CHARACTERS, CULTURE, COMMERCE, ... AND CABIN

Sheridan has been home to many talented artists and photographers over the years. Painters Bill Gollings, Hans Kleiber, and Bernard Thomas left their marks as they captured the essence of the heroic West. Photographers captured the elusive shadows of history as well, and Elsa Spear ranks at the top of list in Sheridan. Born into a ranching family in 1896, Elsa and her sister Jessamine learned photography from their mother, Virginia. The family's dude ranch business gave Elsa the opportunity to go where the pictures were, in the majestic Big Horn Mountains, on working ranches, or around her American Indian neighbors, the Crow.

With five daughters to raise, Elsa Spear used her photographic skill to supplement the family's income and turned her home into a photography studio, complete with enlarger, right in the kitchen. In fact, a hole cut in the kitchen ceiling facilitated raising the device for large prints. The girls knew that when the red safelight was on, their mother was working.

Elsa Spear is best known for four collections of her photographs that represent life in the Big Horn Mountain region. The Indians series shows some of the Sioux survivors of the Battle of the Little Bighorn and includes the photograph called "Burying the Hatchet" with a handshake between Gen. Edward Godfrey and the Sioux, White Bull. The Bighorns series shows the idyllic and rugged beauty of the mountains and lakes in the region. Ranch Life features scenes of working cowboys, and Times to Remember covers the special and everyday aspects of life in the area.

Many historians, amateur and professional, have dedicated their lives to preserving history in the Sheridan area. Mark Badgett, with his dear friend Elsa Spear Byron, was one of those. Mark and his mule Jezebel traveled up and down the Bozeman Trail searching for the remnants of history that its many travelers left behind. Vie Willits Garber of Big Horn was another chronicler of the area's history.

When lifelong friends Joe Medicine Crow and Glenn Sweem played "cowboys and Indians," Joe told Glenn that he wanted to play the cowboy for a change. Joe is an author, anthropologist, Crow tribal elder, and a great contributor and friend to the historical community. Glenn was a founder of the Wyoming Archaeological Society, president of the Sheridan County Historical Society, and instrumental in saving the Sheridan Inn. (Photograph by Scott Burgan.)

What became of Sheridan's oldest structures? Big Horn founder O. P. Hanna and Herman Henschke operated their grocery and confectionary store in the old J. H. Conrad Building from 1891 to 1901. This building is the only false-fronted structure remaining and one of two of Sheridan's earliest. The other is Henry Held's 1884 home on Main and Works Streets.

The store that opened on Sheridan's Main Street in 1883 has housed a number of different businesses, including Mrs. P. A. Campbell's Millinery and Dan's Western Wear. The Hospital Pharmacy has occupied the store since the 1980s, and the false front is adorned with a Bernard Thomas mural that depicts the J. H. Conrad store, its original business.

When Sheridan County's young men went to war, few were left behind to harvest the sugar beets. In the nearby town of Clearmont, German POWs helped win the beet harvest or "campaigns." Many of the local beet farmers like John Fowler (on the truck's hood) were of Russian-German descent, still spoke German, and supervised the POWs. The machines that made beet farming viable everywhere else did not work in the area's rocky soil, and the beet industry around Sheridan ceased in the 1950s.

Progress and time marches on, and the old Sheridan Roller Mills had to be torn down to make way for a flood-control project in 1962. George Grunkemeyer of Vacationland Studios captured the action right across the street from his home. Another mill, opened in 1921, was the largest milling plant in Wyoming. Relying on local production, the Sheridan Flouring Mills produced Best Out West flour and Tomahawk Feeds.

In 1984, the cousin of Sheridan's own earl of Portsmouth came for a visit. That cousin happened to be the queen of England. Her Royal Highness visited one of Sheridan's most beloved establishments, the Ritz Sporting Goods, and received a fly-fishing rod for Prince Philip from proprietor Sam Mavrakis. The queen also visited King's Saddlery and the Maverick Supper Club, and her visit is fondly remembered by many Sheridan residents.

The lovely house that John Loucks built for his family was on the northwest corner of Loucks and Brooks Streets. It was occupied by the family until the 1920s. When his wife, Annie, passed away, John remarried, moving to California shortly thereafter. The house was torn down in the 1950s and was replaced by the telephone company building.

It was finally time to tear down the old Sheridan brewery. It had seen much success, and in 1954, the Sheridan Brewery became the first company in the United States to bottle its flat-topped cans. With production larger than any other plant in America, the Can-a-Pop Beverage Company quickly became the leading producer of canned soft drinks. Franchises sprang up in Los Angeles and Compton, California, and Peoria, Illinois.

As quickly as Can-a-Pop bubbled to the top, it just as quickly fizzled out. Once again, brands like Coca Cola, Pepsi, Fanta, and Nehi with national recognition and advertising edged out the local, hometown soda. The brewery was torn down in 1994, and Whitney Commons Park has taken its place.

If the building on the right looks familiar, it should. It is the Bank of Sheridan that was moved to Loucks Street when a new bank replaced it. The building continued as the home of the Sheridan Banking Company, and pioneer banker E. A. Whitney lived upstairs until his death in 1917.

Later several businesses, including an insurance office and a ballet studio, occupied the structure. When the third First National bank was built in 1970, the little bank had to give way to a parking garage, which replaced it and the Carnegie Library.

When it looked like E. A. Whitney's bank would be demolished, Elsa Spear Byron reminded everyone that the bank had been made from the logs of the Mandel Cabin and that it was the most significant structure in Sheridan's history. The building then became the property of the National Society of the Colonial Dames in America in the State of Wyoming, who saw to its restoration.

In 1977, the bank was dismantled, and the cabin was rebuilt with its original logs. The Sheridan County Historical Society owned John B. Kendrick's Trail End at the time, and the society gave the cabin a home in Trail End's backyard. Ownership of Trail End transferred to the state of Wyoming, and the cabin no longer fit Trail End's interpretive plan. In 2003, the cabin was moved again.

Banker E. A. Whitney's trust, Whitney Benefits, Inc., had just constructed a new park on the old Sheridan Brewery property, and this would be the old cabin's new home. This land happened to be near the spot on the banks of Big Goose Creek where George Mandel built the cabin and where John Loucks sketched a town's plat that he named Sheridan.

In 2005, the granddaughter of John D. Loucks, Margery Loucks Masters, and other Loucks descendants commissioned a bronze of the town's founding father. Local sculptor Gerold Smiley created the statue, which was installed near the steps of the Sheridan City Hall. The new Sheridan Cornet Band provided music from the 1880s for the dedication. Margery, shown here, passed away at age 95 on October 6, 2005.

BIBLIOGRAPHY

Atkins, Patti. *Reflections of the Inn*. Sheridan, WY: Hawks Press, 1994.

Dippie, Brian W. "'The Thrillin'est Fight Ever!' Sheridan Re-enacts Custer's Last Stand." *Annals of Wyoming*. 54.2 (Fall, 1982).

Doyle, Susan Badger. *Stagecoach Lines in Sheridan County, 1878–1894*. Sheridan, WY: Sheridan County Historic Preservation Commission, 1997.

Garber, Vie Willits. *Big Horn Pioneers*. Lovell, WY: Mountain States Printing, 1985.

Georgen, Cynde A. *One Cowboy's Dream: John Kendrick, His Family, Home, and Ranching Empire*. Virginian Beach, VA: The Donning Company Publishers, 2004.

Granum, Robert M. *The History of the Tongue River Tie Flume*. Sheridan, WY: Sheridan County Library Foundation, Inc., 1990.

Hunter, Deck. *Big Horn City, Wyoming Territory, Volume 4: The News*. Casper, WY: Hawks Book Company, 1993.

King, Bucky. *The Dude Connection: A Brief History of Dude Ranching in Sheridan and Buffalo, Wyoming and Birney, Montana*. Laramie, WY: Jelm Mountain Press, 1893.

_____. *The History of Big Horn Polo*. Sheridan, WY: Still Sailing Publications, 1987.

McPherren, Ida. *Empire Builders, A History of the Founding of Sheridan*. Sheridan, WY: Star Publishing Company, 1942.

Monroe, Kathy. *Sheridan Pictorial History*. Sheridan, WY: Sheridan County Fulmer Public Library, 1981.

McWilliams, Mary Ellen and Cynde A. Georgen, eds. *Around the Edges of Sheridan County History*. Sheridan, WY: Sheridan County Historical Society, 2005.

Popovich, Charles W. Sheridan *Wyoming: Selected Historical Articles*. Sheridan, WY: Self Published, 1997.

Sheridan County Extension Homemakers Council. *Sheridan County Heritage Book*. Pierre, SD: The State Publishing Company, 1983.

The *Sheridan Press*. Various articles, 1950–1970.

Visit us at
arcadiapublishing.com

CPSIA information can be obtained
at www.ICGtesting.com
Printed in the USA
BVHW021520121222
654037BV00004B/97